CAREER AS A
LAWYER
TAX ATTORNEY

TAXATION IS HOW THE GOVERNMENT COLLECTS the money needed to provide services to its citizens. The most commonly recognized taxes are income tax and sales tax. There are also many other forms of taxes that we do not notice or think about, such as use taxes, real estate taxes, gas taxes, trade tariffs, and "sin taxes" (taxes on alcohol, cigarettes, gambling, etc.). Taxes are not voluntary, but rather enforced under various laws. Those laws are extremely complex and in constant flux.

Tax attorneys have extensive knowledge of the Tax Code and they follow the changes as they develop. They are able to identify key deductions, exemptions, and credits that could make a significant impact on an individual or company's tax obligation. They help people, businesses, and organizations minimize taxes without getting into legal trouble.

The IRS is responsible for administering and enforcing the laws regarding federal income tax. There are numerous other authorities that create and enforce tax laws and collect tax revenues, ranging from the smallest townships to the federal government. They include agencies, transit districts, utility companies, schools, and more. Tax attorneys can represent clients, both individuals and organizations, before any taxing body. They negotiate with tax authorities or defend clients in court if a dispute with government tax officials arises.

Most people think of tax attorneys in connection with tax evasion or audits. Tax attorneys do represent individuals in those situations, but most deal with organizations, which may be businesses or nonprofit groups. As complex as the tax code is for individuals, it is many times more complicated for businesses. It is such a broad area of the law that tax attorneys often focus in a specific area, such as international tax, partnership tax, tax litigation, executive compensation, pension funding, or tax-exempt organizations.

It takes considerable education and training to become a tax attorney. A law degree is the minimum requirement and a master's degree in tax law is recommended. Those who make it through the seven or eight years of intense study will find that the job outlook and the earnings are excellent. Highly competent tax attorneys are in constant demand, and it is a very flexible career path. Tax attorneys can join the in-house staff of a big corporation, work at a law firm or accounting firm, or go into business for themselves. Wherever they choose to practice, they will be rewarded with six figure incomes and a very satisfying career.

YOUR ASSIGNMENT

THERE IS MUCH THAT ASPIRING TAX LAWYERS can do to start preparing for this career while in high school. The first step is to make sure you fulfill college entrance requirements, which generally include four years of math, science, and English. Beyond the basics, the most useful courses are those that will help you develop precise writing, advanced reading comprehension, critical thinking, and organized research skills.

Pay particular attention to writing and research skills. Tax attorneys spend most of their time combing through the massive tax code and preparing complex transactions and tax opinions. In this field, success requires strong, persuasive writing to help clients come out on top. Classes in political science, economics, psychology, and computer science are also good choices for developing analytical thought processes.

Beyond the regular school day, extracurricular debate programs can provide valuable practice in making persuasive arguments. Get training in spreadsheet software, such as Microsoft Excel. There are plenty of free courses online to choose from.

Spend some time investigating the realities of this career. Ask your guidance counselor to help you set up a job shadow, or contact practicing tax attorneys yourself. When you are meeting tax attorneys, be sure to ask them what they like and do not like about their job, what their daily schedule looks like, and what advice they might have for someone who wants to be in their position someday. Spend as much time as you can observing these professionals at work. The more you see, the more you will know if this is the right career choice for you.

HISTORY OF THE CAREER

AS LONG AS THERE HAVE BEEN CIVILIZED SOCIETIES with the need to provide services for the citizenry, as well as comfort for the rulers, there have been taxes. The Pharaohs of Ancient Egypt had tax collectors, known as scribes. One of the many taxes was imposed on cooking oil. This proved to be so lucrative, it led to the first known tax audits. Tax scribes audited households to ensure that citizens were not cheating on their taxes by recycling oil.

The Ancient Greeks levied taxes known as *eisphora* to cover the costs during wartime. Unlike most societies, the Greeks rescinded the tax once the emergency was over and even used any wartime gains to refund the tax.

The rulers of the Roman Empire were enthusiastic about the idea of taxes. The first taxes related to trade were Rome's customs duties on imports called *portoria*. Other firsts, mostly conceived and implemented by Caesar Augustus and Julius Caesar, included property tax, sales tax, marriage tax (for NOT getting married), inheritance tax, poll tax, slave tax, and religious tax (on Jews only). Tax revolts were attempted, but were quickly crushed by the massive and ruthless Roman army.

Great Britain was also keen on taxation, which led to

numerous ugly rebellions, including the American Revolution. One of the more colorful stories was that of Lady Godiva, whose husband, the Earl of Mercia, had imposed high taxes on the residents of medieval Coventry. After she repeatedly pleaded for him to lessen the people's burden, he agreed only if she would ride a horse, naked, through the town at midday. Lady Godiva called his bluff and became an instant populist heroine. Historians say the incident never actually occurred, but it lived on in legend as a metaphor for how people felt about oppressive taxation.

The British invented the income tax system as we know it today. It began with Charles I imposing income taxes on the wealthy, office holders, and the clergy. The poor paid little or no taxes. The idea of a progressive tax on those with the ability to pay did not sit well with Parliament, whose members were all subject to the tax. As a result, the King was beheaded and Parliament changed the rules, extracting more funds by increasingly taxing the poor. The regressive taxation, along with additional taxation on essential commodities, led to the Smithfield riots in 1647 and the legend of Robin Hood.

Colonial America

Before the American colonies became an independent nation, the British Parliament imposed all taxes. Revenues were collected primarily through tariffs and duties on particular items, such as liquor, tobacco, sugar, and legal documents. More and more taxes were piled on through various Parliamentary Acts in order to cover the costs of maintaining the military presence that purportedly protected the colonies. The colonists protested loudly, "No taxation without representation" and boycotted some British imports. Parliament was not deterred, and placed additional taxes on common products imported into the colonies, such as lead, paper, paint, glass, and tea. In order to avoid any more boycotts, the new laws did not tax people directly. Instead, they were handled as trade tariffs, collected from the ship's captain when he unloaded the cargo.

The final attempt by Parliament to impose new taxes was the passage of the Tea Act, which received royal assent in 1773. Its purpose was to undercut tea smugglers to the benefit of the British-owned East India Company. The result, however, led to the undoing of British rule over the American Colonies. American colonists protested by dumping many chests of tea into Boston Harbor. This action, known as the Boston Tea Party, was met with harsh retaliation, and the conflict escalated to war in 1775.

Taxation in a New Nation

America was free of direct taxation for much of its early history, but the new nation, like all societies, needed money to function. The founding fathers started with excise taxes on specific items in order to cover the costs of certain activities. These are taxes paid when purchases are made of specific goods, such as gasoline. Excise taxes are often included in the price of the product. There are also excise taxes on activities, such as on wagering or on highway usage by trucks.

To cover the war debt of the American Revolution, Alexander Hamilton proposed a tax on distilled spirits. After some debate, Congress agreed. Because American whiskey was by far the most popular distilled beverage of the time, it was widely known as the whiskey tax. In 1794, Pennsylvania farmers reacted with fury, burning down tax collectors' houses and tarring and feathering any collectors who dared come to collect. Many of the resisters were war veterans who believed it was a matter of principle, in particular, taxation without local representation. The Whiskey Rebellion ended when President Washington sent troops to end the revolt. It demonstrated that the new federal government had the ability to suppress violent resistance to its tax laws. However, the whiskey tax proved too difficult to collect and was eventually repealed during the Jefferson administration.

Other indirect taxes imposed in post-revolutionary America, such as the estate tax, gift tax, and federal property tax, arose from the need to finance wars. There were often rebellions, but none were significant or effective.

Federal Income Tax

The first personal income tax suggested in the United States was during the War of 1812. The tax was based on the British Tax Act of 1798 and applied progressive rates to income. This proposal went nowhere, but President Lincoln signed the Tax Act of 1862 in order to finance the Civil War. This was a temporary income tax that was met with little resistance, but compliance was low. It was modified and finally repealed in 1872, replaced by stiff tariffs that served as the major revenue source for the nation until 1913. The Internal Revenue Service was established at the same time the Tax Act of 1862 was enacted, and remained active even after its repeal. It grew to become the premiere collector of taxes and the largest employer of tax attorneys in the US.

The 16th Amendment, which was ratified in 1913, provided Congress the authority to tax the citizenry on income from whatever source derived. It laid the foundation for the first permanent personal income tax. Interestingly, corporate income taxes were enacted a few years earlier, in 1909. Business owners, not the corporations themselves, were taxed.

America's first citizens enjoyed few to no taxes, Over time, taxes were added, increased, and occasionally repealed (and replaced by more expansive versions) to give us the complex tax regime we have today. The federal income tax is but one of many taxes Americans are subjected to. Throughout the 20th century, numerous kinds of taxes were added on things we use everyday, such as gas and energy taxes, aviation taxes, and telecommunications taxes. Some taxes were added to support social safety net programs, like Social Security and Medicare. Others extracted portions of investment income, like capital gains and dividend taxes. The federal government is not the only collector of taxes. Every state also taxes its residents, primarily through sales tax and income tax.

The history of taxation in America began with the colonial protest against British taxation policy in the 1760s, which led directly to the American Revolution and the founding of a new nation. History is full of tax rebellions – nobody likes taxes and nobody wants to pay one cent more than absolutely necessary. Riots and revolutions may be history, but Americans can still resist over-taxation with some expert help. The federal income tax code started out as a relatively simple statement and has mushroomed into 75,000 pages. Ordinary citizens are supposed to comply with every detail, but how realistic is that? People get behind in their taxes or make mistakes that result in legal troubles. Others need help planning for the future or starting a business. The need for professional help from tax attorneys has never been greater.

WHERE YOU WILL WORK

TAX ATTORNEYS CAN BE FOUND WORKING in a wide variety of practice settings. In the private sector, the largest employers of tax attorneys are the large accounting firms. Other employers include large law firms, boutique tax services, corporations, and nonprofit organizations. Large law firms are typically divided into multiple departments that each focuses on certain areas of the law. Tax attorneys usually work in the departments that specialize in estate planning, employee benefits, and individual or business tax issues.

In the public sector, tax attorneys are employed by tax courts and government agencies, both federal and state. Not surprisingly, the Internal Revenue Service (IRS) employs more tax attorneys than any other single entity. The IRS is divided into many specialized departments. Some are based entirely in Washington, DC, while others are scattered throughout the country in dozens of field offices. Each department has a substantial staff of tax attorneys (roughly 50 to 100) that meet particular qualifications. For example, the more than 50 attorneys working in the Financial Institutions and Products Division of the Associate Chief Counsel are experts in financial products such as stocks and insurance. Most work in the National Office in Washington, DC. The more than 90 attorneys working in the Criminal Tax Division, on the other hand, may be assigned to any of the 30 offices across the country. Their expertise is in criminal investigation and forensic accounting related to money laundering, currency issues, fraud, and other tax-related crimes committed domestically or abroad.

Many tax attorneys are self-employed, working in solo or small group practices. For them, they are "employed" by clients. Clients are much the same as those they work for when employed as a full-time salaried staff member of a law firm or accounting service. The largest group of clients are individuals, who may have serious tax problems or need help with estate planning. Other clients can include small to medium sized companies, government agencies (usually at the state or local level), nonprofits, healthcare organizations, private foundations, and trade associations.

Tax attorneys work in formal, professional offices. Most tax attorneys enjoy a normal work schedule. Solo practitioners, however, often work long hours. Weekly hours can easily surpass 40 hours when they are working on a major case.

THE WORK YOU WILL DO

TAXATION IS A SIMPLE IDEA. Money is needed to fund the services that government provides. Historically, taxes were first collected on a temporary basis to finance wars. Today, however, the array of government services is vast. It takes more than $4 trillion to cover the costs of building roads and bridges, educating millions of school children, operating the justice system, maintaining a national defense, ensuring a clean environment, and providing social services like healthcare and Social Security. These essential functions of government are all paid for with taxes, which amounts to a substantial financial obligation for individuals and companies. The idea that started out so simple is now anything but simple.

There are many different kinds of taxes imposed at the federal, state, county, and municipal levels. In addition to the most commonly known – income tax and sales tax – there are taxes, fees, and tariffs on a wide range of activities and products. Add to that the multiple types of exemptions, deductions, and some would say "loopholes," and the result is a mind-boggling system. It is impossible for the average citizen to make sense of the highly technical statutes that make up our current tax regime. Tax attorneys are needed to help clients, both individuals and companies, navigate this complex area of law.

Job Duties of a Tax Attorney

The work tax attorneys do can be quite varied. On any one day, time may be spent structuring an acquisition, writing a tax opinion, negotiating tax relief, representing an individual accused of tax fraud, or giving general tax advice to a new client. Tax attorneys typically work with high net worth individuals and corporations, providing guidance related to all areas of tax law. They monitor legislative developments on a daily basis and advise clients of the potential impact pending legislation may have on their personal finances and businesses.

Benjamin Franklin is famous for saying that only two things in life are certain: death and taxes. Tax attorneys work on trying to ease the financial burdens associated with both. The wealthier the individual, the more essential this work becomes. Tax attorneys use trusts, gifts, investment strategies, and a variety of tax planning structures to reduce the burdens of income taxes and estate taxes.

For small businesses and corporations, tax attorneys use a number of tactics to minimize tax exposure. This generally involves determining the tax consequences of business plans and decisions. In the corporate arena, tax attorneys often work hand-in-hand with corporate in-house counsel. Tax attorneys must review each financial decision made by a corporation. From financing debt to depreciation of assets, there are always tax implications to consider.

Much of the corporate work done by tax attorneys is related to transactions. Common examples of transactional work include mergers and acquisitions, real estate investment trusts, and investment funds. The work generally involves analyzing, creating, and implementing complex transactions from the tax perspective. Tax attorneys counsel corporate clients on the potential tax consequences of specific transactions, and monitor changes in the tax code that might require a direction change. More experienced tax attorneys provide more expert advice directly to clients on discrete tax issues. These senior attorneys review tax disclosures in securities offerings, structure joint ventures, review and negotiate the tax provisions in loan agreements and financial products, and draft tax opinions.

Ideally, clients do not end up in court, but plans can backfire and mistakes can be made. Some tax attorneys specialize in litigating the tax treatment of controversial tax positions. Tax litigation can be in Tax Court, Federal District Court, or the Court of Federal Claims. In the event of tax fraud, cases may also end up in criminal court. Tax attorneys might also appear before federal, state or local taxing authorities.

Because most taxes are collected by the IRS, that is the most common battleground for tax attorneys. The IRS is somewhat particular about who can represent a taxpayer should a problem or audit arise. Attorneys make the list of approved counsel, along with certified public accountants and enrolled agents. Since attorneys are considered to have rights to "unlimited" representation of clients, they do not have to be the ones who prepared the tax return in question in order to appear before the

IRS or in a federal court on someone's behalf.

Most tax attorneys never see the inside of a courtroom or even interact with a judge. Instead, the work is all about research. In fact, tax attorneys throughout their careers devote more of their time to research than attorneys in other practice areas. A typical day usually begins with reading daily tax publications. This might seem dull, but it is at the heart of the tax attorney's job. While it is a challenge to keep up with the never-ending changes and developments in tax law, it is also an opportunity for younger attorneys to know as much about a specific issue as their senior colleagues.

Despite the thousands of pages in the Internal Revenue Code and Treasury Regulations, there are still many unanswered questions about how the tax rules apply to a specific situation. Some attorneys specialize in tax-related controversies. Individuals or businesses may be subject to investigation or an audit, or they may have attempted to shelter or exempt money from tax collection in a way disallowed by the IRS or other tax collection entities. Experts in tax controversies may represent clients during audits or negotiate with the IRS. This usually involves direct communication with government attorneys and auditors. There is usually much research required, followed by writing ruling requests, comments on proposed Treasury Regulations, questions under existing regulations, and tax opinions. The most serious tax treatment issues may be heard in the US District Court.

Duties will often depend on where attorneys work and their level of experience. In a big law firm junior attorneys work under the supervision of more senior attorneys in the tax group. The senior attorneys work directly with clients, while the juniors conduct research and provide support. Both junior and senior tax associates consult and interact with other departments, the opposition's in-house counsel, and the client's accountants.

As tax lawyers at large firms gain experience, they often specialize and develop expertise in an area, such as financial products or mergers and acquisitions (M&A). It is actually more challenging to work at a firm with a small tax department. If there are only one or two tax attorneys on staff, it becomes necessary to handle any and every tax question, and advise on any type of transaction that comes up. That can be quite a challenge given the complexity of tax law.

Specialties

Tax law is a broad area that covers a variety of work, such as general corporate tax, executive compensation, tax litigation, international tax planning, exempt organizations, and municipal finance. A few of the most common specialties include tax planning for nonprofits, employee benefit plans, and estate planning.

Tax planning for tax-exempt organizations covers a wide territory. There are many kinds of exempt groups, such as charities, private foundations, fraternal beneficiary organizations, volunteer groups, schools, arts organizations, veterans organizations, and various benefit trusts, to name a few. Each of these has special tax planning guidelines and concerns. The federal and state requirements for establishing and maintaining their tax-exempt status are quite complex. Tax attorneys who specialize in this area have the expertise to guide them through the procedures necessary to gain and maintain their tax-exempt status.

Employee benefits are a complicated subject that requires expertise in pension, profit-sharing, employee stock ownership, and 401(k) plans. The federal government has reporting and disclosure requirements that govern the funding and administration of pension plans. Tax attorneys make sure those requirements are adhered to. They also design and administer employee benefit plans while monitoring the long-range financial implications resulting from such plans.

Estate planning is one of the biggest specialties. Tax attorneys in this area help individuals plan the distribution of their estate either prior to or upon their death. There are numerous tax consequences that stem from the use of gifts and trusts to minimize tax liabilities upon the transfer of the estate. This is not a subject of concern solely for the wealthy. Regardless of income level, a will should be used to avoid probate, and life insurance is an excellent way to distribute tax-free cash to heirs. Tax attorneys can help design and execute the most advantageous plan.

STORIES OF TAX ATTORNEYS AT WORK

I Work at an International Law Firm

"Many tax attorneys have a background in accounting or business. I am one of them. I earned an accounting degree before entering law school and was hired by a major accounting firm through an on-campus interview. It is not necessary to have a degree in accounting, but it definitely has advantages. Employers like mine scour law school campuses in search of third year students who studied accounting as undergraduates. They also encourage those who haven't yet chosen tax law as their specialty by offering internships to second and third year law students.

Most tax attorneys didn't know while in law school that they were going to end up practicing tax law. The decision usually comes after being exposed to the field through internships. I recommend taking a basic tax class in law school to learn what tax attorneys do. Once you start practicing, you can pursue a master's degree – LL.M. in tax. You don't need an LL.M. to start practicing. I went to night classes while working full time and it worked out great. During my night classes I learned advanced legal concepts and I was able to apply those concepts on the job the next day."

I Am a Tax Controversy Specialist

"My clients are primarily large multinational corporations. The bigger the company, the more complex and vexing the tax profile becomes. At the international level, it is often too complicated even for the very sophisticated in-house tax staffs at these companies. That is when they come to me for help. We work as a team to investigate and solve the problem. Typical cases arise when an IRS agent says the tax obligation should be adjusted upward. When this happens, it is no small matter. Adjustments can range from $10 million on the low side to more than $100 million. My job is to resist the adjustment. Sometimes that means litigating the issue in federal tax court.

There is no typical day in my job, but there is a lot of interaction with various people. I can spend an entire day on the phone with a client, developing a strategy. Most days it's a combination of meetings, interviewing witnesses, and negotiating with an IRS agent or appeals officer. My knowledge of tax law and negotiating skills are vital, but people skills are just as important. In fact, many firms are placing much greater emphasis on communications and interpersonal skills. If you have those skills, you will always be in demand. There are more opportunities than ever for staff-level attorneys to get out in front with clients."

PERSONAL QUALIFICATIONS

WHAT DOES IT TAKE TO BE A TAX ATTORNEY? Solid accounting and math skills are a must, along with the knowledge of the technical possibilities. Just as important is an analytical mind, insatiable curiosity, and creativity. The difference between an average tax attorney and a great one is the ability to think outside the box. Clients seek out the services of tax attorneys because they have complex problems that require innovative, yet practical solutions. Critical thinking and creativity are a winning combination. If you enjoy challenging yourself intellectually like this, tax law could be a good fit.

Research skills, both legal and factual, are vital in every branch of the law. On television, attorneys spend most of their time going head to head with judges or chasing down bad guys. The reality for attorneys in the real world is quite different. For tax attorneys, the bulk of the work revolves around studying tax law. You cannot just read it once either, since it constantly changes. On average, tax attorneys spend several hours every day learning what is looming, what has been implemented, and how to anticipate and plan for any changes. You also need to be good at factual development, which means digging into what your client is telling you to get to the details that matter. Without good facts, you cannot put together a good proposal or winning argument.

Communications skills, both spoken and written, are also needed. As a tax attorney, you will be trained to understand a very complicated tax code along with all its ramifications. A great tax attorney is able to simplify complex issues and make them understandable to anyone. Excellent writing skills are also needed. This job involves copious writing, from general tax opinions, to court arguments, to reports on the tax consequences of future strategies and transactions. If you do not like to write, this may not be the right career for you.

Successful tax attorneys have excellent interpersonal skills. They work closely with their clients on a daily basis, which means they must be able to form relationships. They also need to work well in teams or with other professionals. Tax law often intersects with other areas of the law or related professional fields. Tax law is more likely to be interactive and team oriented.

People come to tax attorneys with serious problems that may have them stressed out or scared. They need to know that they can depend on you to help them avoid financial disaster. It is not enough to be very bright if you lack the personal skills to make clients comfortable with your advice. Part of instilling confidence and trust in people is how you speak and present yourself. Do not let your ego get in the way and do not be phony. The ability to inject humor, personal stories, and anecdotes into discussions is critically important. You must also have a sincere interest in your clients and their situations. Try to learn as much as you can about them, their business, and their goals for the future. Do not hesitate to ask questions. The more questions you ask, the more apparent it will be that you are dedicated to finding the best solutions.

The ability to simplify is essential. Tax law and relating rules are often very complex. A great tax lawyer has the skills to simplify complex issues into understandable formats. A bad tax lawyer tries to impress clients by talking over their heads or getting into nuances that the clients do not need to understand.

Also important is thinking outside the box. Clients do not want or need to know all the technical details, but they want to know that you are thinking in different ways than other attorneys they have talked with. Taking something you know in one area and applying it in a substantially different way is a very important skill.

ATTRACTIVE FEATURES

THE SALARY AND BONUSES PAID to tax attorneys are great and they get bigger each year. Tax law is a field that has much more to offer than good money. In survey after survey, tax attorneys talk about the many ways their practice is rewarding. What these professionals like most about the work is the intellectual challenge. Tax attorneys are smart people who enjoy giving their brains a good workout every day. They do not ever want to get stuck doing mundane, mindless tasks. While most of us would find the constantly changing rules frustrating, tax attorneys relish keeping up and learning something new each day.

Tax attorneys do not ever have to confront boredom. From the outside, this career may look like every day would be the same, but there is actually considerable variety. It is a complex field that allows tax attorneys to expand their expertise each day. There is a real range of projects and plenty of other sharp professionals to collaborate with. Most tax attorneys have a mix of cases that provide individual client interaction as well as more team working environments. Clients come in all varieties, too. They could range from the average citizen to sophisticated mover and shakers, or from small mom and pop businesses to multinational corporations.

Tax attorneys are much more than number crunchers. There is constant interaction with other people. Perhaps the most enjoyable part of the work is teaming up with other professionals to solve problems. The relationships you will have with the people you work with will be very rewarding. It is fun to work side by side with colleagues who are really smart and talented. These people are usually interested in friendship outside the workplace as well as the professional environment. Tax attorneys also enjoy forming strong relationships with their clients. It is not unusual to have clients essentially for life, and you become more like a friend of the family than just the "tax person." Those who deal with small businesses often get to know more than one generation of the family that owns the business.

Tax attorneys have an interesting work life, and they also get to enjoy their personal time, too. Work-life balance is inherent in this field. In fact, tax attorneys enjoy some of the most life-friendly working patterns in the legal industry. The hours for most are 9 to 6, with ample time for good lunches and trips to the gym, and still make it home in time to sit down to dinner with the family. It can be a very civilized branch of the profession.

The work is very satisfying. Tax attorneys help their clients solve complex legal and financial problems. At the very least, you can help them save money. But your efforts can offer a great deal more value to clients. Some people have suffered severe damage to their businesses, personal financial health, and even their reputations due to missteps in handling tax issues. It does not necessarily mean they have done anything wrong or illegal. Often the losses are the result of perfectly legal tax plans that were poorly executed by a layperson without the expertise of a tax attorney. You can be the legal knight in shining armor, fixing their problems and saving their financial life or business. The opportunity to make such a positive difference in people's lives is a great motivation to do this work.

UNATTRACTIVE ASPECTS

TAX ATTORNEYS ARE SMART PEOPLE who enjoy the intellectual challenge of this career. However, the need to keep up with nonstop changes, new developments, and strategies is relentless. It can be difficult completing all the necessary reading and learning while also handling the day-to-day client work. It is also a challenge for solo practitioners who must spend a fair amount of time on non-billable professional reading.

Depending on where you work, this can be a stressful job. Stress shows up most often in large law firms where associates are constantly under pressure. Workloads for associates are heavy and they must get every detail correct. There is no room for even a small mistake because mistakes in the world of tax lax can be quite costly. Solo practitioners usually experience the least stress because they have more control over their schedule and workload.

Tax attorneys do not typically have the same demanding schedules that corporate or litigation lawyers do. The situation can be different at large law firms where long hours and sudden demands are common. Rush research assignments are usually dropped on the junior associates. Corporate taxes, mergers, and other transactions often have deadlines that can mean long hours and working at home on the weekends.

Billable hours are a big headache for every attorney, and it is no exception for those working in tax law. Big law firms and accounting firms often keep track of their attorneys' time right down to 5-minute increments. Imagine having to account for everything you do and determine whether that 5 minutes you just worked was billable to a client or not. Smaller employers are a little less strict, and solo practitioners usually do estimated billings or amounts agreed upon in advance. Still, there is no escaping the need to keep track of how time is spent, and get paid for it, to ensure a firm stays financially healthy.

Are you looking forward to a glamorous career filled with courtroom drama? If so, you will be disappointed. Tax attorneys rarely, if ever, see the inside of actual courtrooms. This is a career that will have you sitting at your desk, peering at a computer, and shuffling papers most of the time. The occasional break comes when meeting with clients or brainstorming with colleagues and others on your team.

EDUCATION AND TRAINING

THE EDUCATIONAL REQUIREMENTS to become a tax attorney are quite substantial, amounting to seven or eight years of academic study. The first four years are devoted to earning a bachelor's degree. Some, but not all, colleges offer pre-law majors for students intending to go to law school, but this is not a prerequisite for law school. As long as you successfully graduate from college with a bachelor's degree, you can major in any subject you want. However, this is a good time to take extra courses in business, economics, and accounting. Many tax attorneys are also certified public accountants (CPAs). Some hold MBAs (Master's in Business Administration), plus a law degree.

The second step is going to law school. Before gaining admission to law school, students must pass the Law School Admission test, commonly referred to as the LSAT. If accepted, they enroll in a Juris Doctor (JD) degree program, which takes about three years of full-time study to complete. Law school starts with core law courses, such as civil procedures, constitutional law, torts, legal methods, and contracts. After covering the basics, students move on to more specialized courses, like limited partnerships, business liquidations, corporations, and bankruptcy. Students can also pursue a particular area of interest or specialization by enrolling in classes like securities regulations, venture capital, or emerging companies. Various tax and accounting courses are available throughout law school and aspiring tax attorneys should take advantage of as many as possible.

The JD degree is the minimum required to work as a tax attorney. Most tax attorneys also have a Master of Laws (LLM) graduate degree in taxation, which is an internationally recognized law degree. While an LLM in taxation is not necessarily required to become a tax attorney, many firms prefer candidates who hold the credential because it indicates the attorney is qualified to work in an advanced, multinational legal environment.

It takes about one year after graduating from law school to complete the LLM degree. It is also possible to study part time or online, but it will take longer. An LLM program can focus on any area of law, but tax law is one of the most challenging. The program is intense and highly focused on specific areas of tax law, such as estate planning, business taxation, or international law. There are also more than 50 courses available in highly-defined subjects, ranging from taxation and transactions, to hedge funds, to comparative tax law. Many LLM students participate in internship programs with government agencies or law firms specializing in corporate tax law.

Licensing

In addition to degree requirements, tax attorneys must also be licensed to practice in their state.

Some states offer further certification of tax attorneys after practicing tax law for a minimum period of time, usually about five years. The experience must be recent and there is an exam to pass. Finally, all attorneys must pass a state bar exam and be admitted to the bar in the state in which they intend to practice. This bar exam usually takes place over multiple days and can be repeated if necessary.

EARNINGS

TAX ATTORNEYS ENJOY A SUBSTANTIAL INCOME with average annual six-figure salaries across the US. Many tax attorneys receive extra income on top of their base salaries, which brings their average total compensation up to $150,000. Average salaries range from $75,000 to $200,000, but profit sharing can amount to as much as $25,000 and bonuses can be anywhere from $5,000 to more than $50,000. That means the total annual earnings could be as high as $250,000.

There are several factors that affect how much an individual might be paid. The main one is the individual's level of experience. Offers to new graduates starting out average roughly $90,000, while successful tax attorneys with at least five years of experience might earn nearly twice as much. Success is often quantified by meeting performance goals, which in turn, results in bonuses that help boost income.

Geography also plays a role in determining income for these careerists. The best paychecks are likely to be found in places where there are Fortune 500 corporate headquarters and financial centers, such as New York and Chicago. Conversely, working in areas where the clientele is comprised mostly of individual taxpayers rather than corporations can mean that salaries are 30 percent lower.

Income for tax attorneys also varies depending on where they work. In the private sector, the worst place to work in terms of salary is a small client tax relief firm that mostly caters to individual customers. There the annual salaries range from $50,000 to $80,000. In the public sector, state government agencies like a comptroller's office or department of revenue typically offer only

$50,000 to $65,000 a year. The news is better at the federal level though. The IRS, which is the nation's largest employer of tax attorneys, is 100 percent better, with yearly pay averaging $125,000. For the financially ambitious tax attorney, there is no arguing with the advantages of working in the corporate world. A typical Blue Chip firm like IBM pays an average $150,000 to its staff tax attorneys. In the financial sector, big players like Morgan Stanley, reward their top tax attorneys with salaries and bonuses topping $350,000 a year.

Benefits can also vary for tax attorneys depending on whether they work for the government, a private business, or themselves. Those who are self-employed must fend for themselves. They must pay for their own health insurance, set up their own retirement plans, and forego any paid sick leave or vacation time. Their salaried colleagues, however, can expect full benefits. The best benefit programs are offered by government agencies, which helps compensate for the typically lower salaries compared to private firms. Government-provided pension plans are particularly attractive. Private firms usually cover all the basics, like medical and dental as well as a finite amount of PTO (paid time off). Plus, the larger the business, the more likely it is that bonuses and profit sharing will enhance your earnings.

OPPORTUNITIES

FUTURE TAX ATTORNEYS CAN LOOK FORWARD to an excellent job outlook. Tax attorneys are in high demand for one very good reason: our tax regime is incredibly complex and it is not getting any simpler. The ever-growing US tax code is currently about 75,000 pages long. It is loaded with details about how individuals, businesses, and exempt organizations are subject to taxes. It contains specific economic and policy directives designed to encourage consumption, imports, and exports of particular products and services. Very few people understand more than a handful of tax code particulars as they exist, and fewer will be aware of changes as they are made. Individuals with the knowledge and expertise necessary to interpret the rules and keep up with the constant changes are sorely needed.

Tax law is one of the most challenging areas of practice, but it is also one of the most in demand specializations. The government will always need money, and taxes are the primary revenue vehicle. Major legislative and regulatory changes take place all the time. Most tax attorneys spend a significant portion of their time monitoring changes in tax regulations and determining how the changes will affect their clients' situations.

One of the most significant changes affecting the tax code in recent years is the Affordable Care Act, which has added an additional 3,000 pages. The IRS is in charge of overseeing compliance with the Act, making this a major new area for tax attorneys. Businesses, in particular, are in need of tax attorneys who have studied healthcare law to help determine their responsibilities.

Tax attorneys have many options with regard to how and where they practice. Many start out working for big law or accounting firms, or government agencies. About one out of four will eventually leave the comfort of salaried employment to start their own firms. Large law firms with multiple departments represent the most common starting point for newly licensed tax attorneys. Some start their first jobs while simultaneously studying for an LLM in tax law. After a few years on the job – five, on average – many will move on to smaller firms, accounting firms, or corporate in-house positions.

There are more tax attorneys employed in Washington, DC than anyplace else. That is because of the many opportunities in tax regulatory work in the nation's capital. It is also home to the largest single employer of tax attorneys, the IRS. Any large city has firms in need of tax attorneys to deal with transactions, business planning, issues related to financial products, and corporate law. Tax attorneys in smaller cities are more likely to be needed to work in the state and local tax (SALT) area. Tax attorneys are also more likely to operate successful solo practices in smaller cities where there is less competition.

The job outlook for general law school graduates is better than that for most other occupations. However, tax law is a specialty with particularly high demand. Those with the necessary expertise to practice in this area will have a very good chance of successfully finding high paying, lasting employment upon graduation. Tax attorneys also have the advantage of being fluent in two professions – law and accounting. Due to the increasing complexity of the tax code that makes the actual filing of taxes more difficult, many accounting and tax preparation firms are hiring tax attorneys to help their clients.

GETTING STARTED

THE KEY TO MAKING YOURSELF VALUABLE in the eyes of potential employers is to get as much experience as you can. Start taking advantage of all the services your school has to offer right away. Clinical programs are among the best services provided by most law schools. These programs are designed to help you gain practical experience by working with real clients on real issues related specifically to tax law. Some law schools also offer tax clinics to the public, which is the kind of training you should not miss out on. You can duplicate this experience volunteering your services to a community based income tax assistance program.

Large law firms will expect to see some work experience in an actual law firm on your résumé. You can get this experience by working as a law clerk or as a summer associate. Just make sure the law firm has a tax practice. Large firms generally hire associates to work during the summer between the second and third year of law school. Smaller firms hire students during the summer, but also offer part-time positions throughout the school year.

Be sure to participate in good internships and externships. This is an exclusive field with enough job openings for every new tax attorney to be assured of full employment. Still, employers naturally want to hire the best and brightest, and that is where internships come in. It is the best way for students to prove themselves.

Internships and externships are also good for making the right connections. The contacts made through these programs often lead to a law graduate's first job as a tax attorney. You can also make good connections through your law school's alumni office. This office can put you in touch with alumni who are doing what you want to do. In addition to possibly alerting you to job openings, these people can provide plenty of useful advice. Take advantage of the opportunity to talk informally to those who are practicing in your areas of interest.

Participate in bar association activities while still in school. Students can usually join bar associations for very low fees. The American Bar Association and other state and local bar associations have sections or committees related to tax law. Look for activities that will put you in touch with people who do the type of tax work you want to do. Let them know you are looking for a position and exchange contact information.

ASSOCIATIONS

- **American Bar Association**
  www.americanbar.org

- **American Academy of Estate Planning Attorneys**
  https://www.aaepa.com

- **National Association of Property Tax Attorneys**
  www.napta.com

- **American Academy of Attorney – CPAs (AAA-CPA)**
  https://www.attorney-cpa.com

- National Association of Tax Professional (NATP)
  https://www.natptax.com

- National Society of Tax Professionals
  https://www.nstp.org

PERIODICAL

- The Tax Lawyer
  https://www.americanbar.org/groups/taxation/publications/tax_lawyer_home.html

Copyright 2019
Institute For Career Research CHICAGO
CAREERS INTERNET DATABASE
www.careers-internet.org

www.ingramcontent.com/pod-product-compliance
Lightning Source LLC
Chambersburg PA
CBHW071203220526
45468CB00003B/1135